Album Art Direction/Design: Jackie Murphy & Nick Gamma
Photography: Reisig & Taylor
Album Artwork: © 1999 Zomba Recording Corporation

Project Manager: Jeannette DeLisa
Book Art Layout: Nancy Rehm

Contents

LARGER THAN LIFE

Words and Music by
BRIAN T. LITTRELL, MAX MARTIN
and KRISTIAN LUNDIN

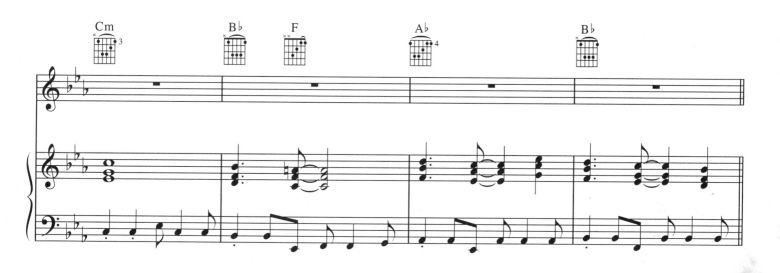

10

(Inst. solo ad lib. . . .

. . . end solo)

Chorus:

keeps us___ a - live.___

All you peo - ple, can't you see, can't you see how___ your love's af - fect - ing our re -

I WANT IT THAT WAY

Words and Music by
MAX MARTIN and
ANDREAS CARLSSON

16

18

SHOW ME THE MEANING
OF BEING LONELY

Words and Music by
MAX MARTIN and HERBERT CRICHLOW

23

IT'S GOTTA BE YOU

Words and Music by
MAX MARTIN and R.J. LANGE

Dance rock ♩ = 120

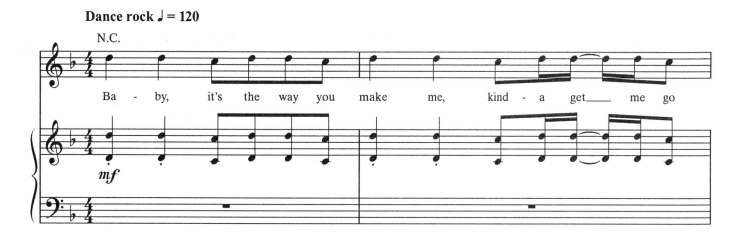

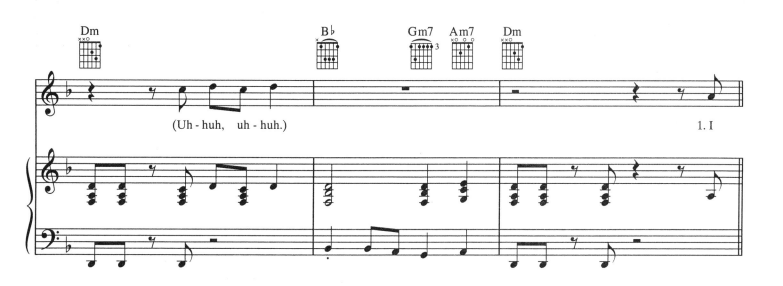

It's Gotta Be You - 6 - 1
PF9916

28

It's Gotta Be You - 6 - 4
PF9916

30

It's Gotta Be You - 6 - 6
PF9916

I NEED YOU TONIGHT

Words and Music by
ANDREW FROMM

Verse 2:
I figured out what to say to you.
But sometimes the words, they, they come out so wrong, oh yes they do.
And I know in time that you will understand.
That what we have is so right this time, and . . .
(To Chorus:)

DON'T WANT YOU BACK

Words and Music by
MAX MARTIN

Don't, don't want you back.

Verse 2:

2. You start - ed go - ing out with so - called_ friends,_

but I was blind and so I lost all com - mon sense.

But there were things that made me re - al - ize,

like all the hun - dred, no, thou - sand lies. Don't want you

42

Chorus:

DON'T WANNA LOSE YOU NOW

Words and Music by
MAX MARTIN

Verse 2:
I've got this feeling you're not gonna stay;
It's burning within me.
The fear of losing, of slipping away,
It just keeps getting closer, baby.
Whatever reason to leave that I've had,
My place was always beside you.
And I wish that I didn't need you so bad;
Your face just won't go away.
(To Chorus:)

THE ONE

Words and Music by
BRIAN T. LITTRELL and MAX MARTIN

56

The One - 6 - 5
PF9916

BACK TO YOUR HEART

Words and Music by
KEVIN RICHARDSON,
GARY BAKER and JASON BLUME

Back to Your Heart - 6 - 1
PF9916

60

§ Chorus:

Back to Your Heart - 6 - 3
PF9916

SPANISH EYES

Words and Music by
ANDREW FROMM and SANDY LINZER

NO ONE ELSE COMES CLOSE

Words and Music by
**GARY BAKER, WAYNE PERRY
and JOE THOMAS**

Chorus:

72

No One Else Comes Close - 6 - 5
PF9916

THE PERFECT FAN

Words and Music by
BRIAN T. LITTRELL and THOMAS L. SMITH

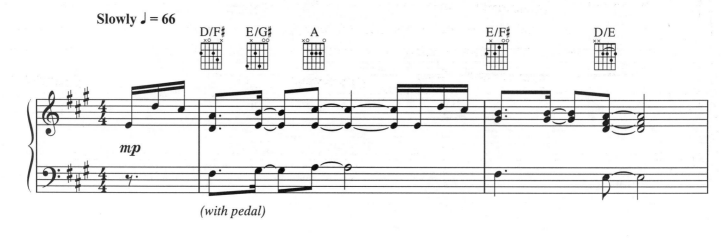

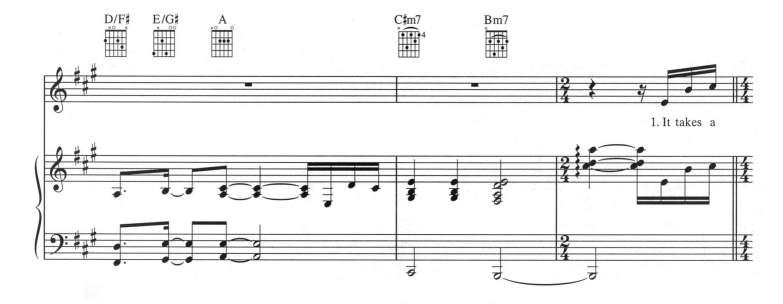

78

The Perfect Fan - 7 - 5
PF9916

Chorus:

proud to say you're mine. You showed me,_ when I was young,_ just how_ to grow._ You

cresc. *poco rit.* *a tempo* **f**

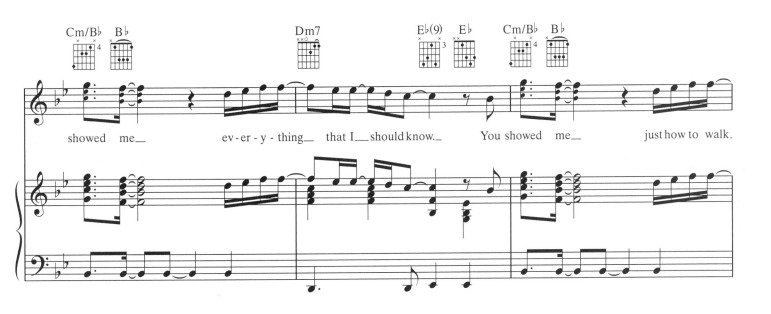

showed me_ ev-er-y-thing_ that I_ should know._ You showed me_ just how to walk_

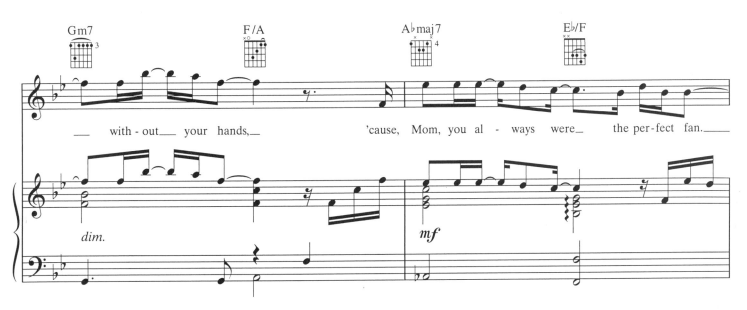

_ with-out_ your hands,_ 'cause, Mom, you al-ways were_ the per-fect fan._

dim. *mf*

80

The Perfect Fan - 7 - 7
PF9916